The Seven Continents

Antarctica

by A. R. Schaefer

Consultant:
Mark Healy
Professor of Geography
William Rainey Harper College
Palatine, Illinois

Capstone press

Mankato, Minnesota

Bridgestone Books are published by Capstone Press,
151 Good Counsel Drive, P.O. Box 669, Mankato, Minnesota 56002.
www.capstonepress.com

Library of Congress Cataloging-in-Publication Data
Schaefer, A. R. (Adam Richard), 1976–
    Antarctica / A. R. Schaefer.
    p. cm.—(Bridgestone books. The seven continents)
    Summary: "Describes the continent of Antarctica, including climate, landforms, plants, animals,
claims, people, as well as Antarctica and the world"—Provided by publisher.
    Includes bibliographical references and index.
    ISBN-13: 978-0-7368-5426-9 (hardcover)
    ISBN-10: 0-7368-5426-6 (hardcover)
    1. Antarctica—Juvenile literature. I. Title. II. Series: Seven continents (Mankato, Minn.)
G863.S31 2006
998—dc22   2005017045

JJ 919.89

Editorial Credits
Becky Viaene, editor; Patrick D. Dentinger, designer; Kim Brown and Tami Collins, map illustrators;
    Wanda Winch, photo researcher; Scott Thoms, photo editor

Photo Credits
Corbis/Galen Rowell, 16, 18, 20
Creatas, 1
Map Resources, cover (background)
Minden Pictures/Colin Monteath, cover (foreground)
Peter Arnold Inc./Kevin Schafer, 12; Norbert Wu, 6
Visuals Unlimited/Gerald & Buff Corsi, 10

1 2 3 4 5 6 11 10 09 08 07 06

Table of Contents

The World's Continents

Antarctica

Little of Antarctica's land can be seen through the thick layer of ice that covers it. But this landmass is the world's fifth-largest continent. It covers about 5.4 million square miles (14 million square kilometers).

Antarctica's cold **climate** makes it very different from other continents. No one lives in Antarctica. But every year, thousands of people from around the world visit Antarctica to do **research**. They want to learn about this cold continent's unique land.

◀ Antarctica is located at the bottom of the earth. It is surrounded by the Southern, or Antarctic, Ocean.

Climate

Antarctica is the coldest place on earth. During winter, temperatures may drop to minus 94 degrees Fahrenheit (minus 70 degrees Celsius). Even in summer, which lasts from November to February, temperatures rarely rise above freezing.

Antarctica is also the world's driest place. Each year, only a few inches of snow fall. Snow has piled up in Antarctica for millions of years. The cold temperatures keep most of the snow from melting.

◀ Powerful winds push snow into large drifts on the world's windiest continent.

Landforms of Antarctica

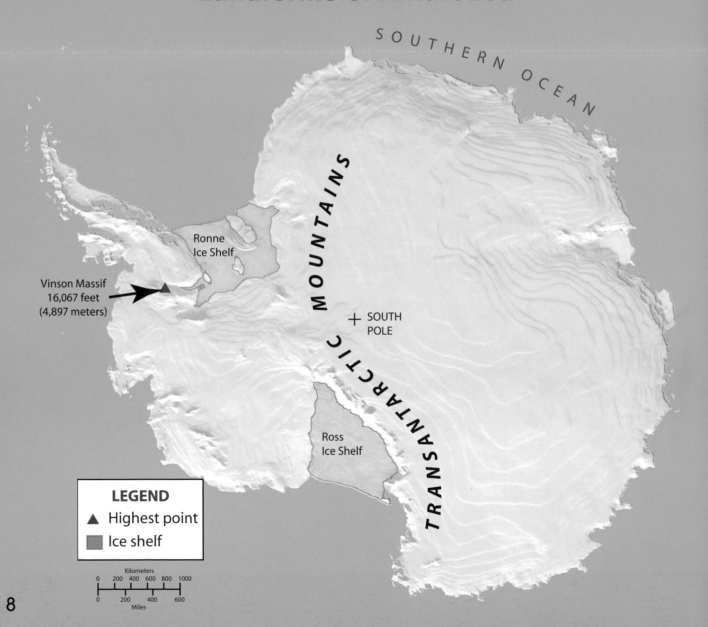

SOUTHERN OCEAN

MOUNTAINS

TRANSANTARCTIC

Ronne
Ice Shelf

Vinson Massif
16,067 feet
(4,897 meters)

+ SOUTH
POLE

Ross
Ice Shelf

LEGEND

▲ Highest point

▊ Ice shelf

Kilometers
0 200 400 600 800 1000

0 200 400 600
Miles

Landforms

Ice isn't found only on Antarctica's land. Huge ice chunks also float around Antarctica in the Southern Ocean. Antarctica's **coast** is connected to two huge floating ice sheets. They are the Ross and Ronne Ice Shelves.

The Transantarctic Mountains divide Antarctica. The world's most southern point, the South Pole, is near these mountains. On the other side of the Transantarctic Mountains lies the tallest mountain in Antarctica, Vinson Massif.

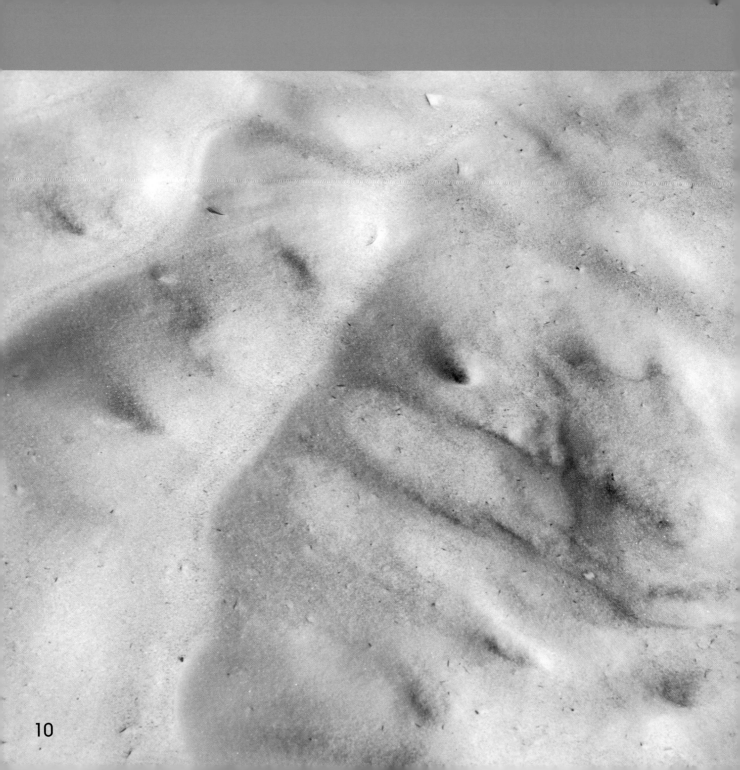

Plants

Few plants can grow in Antarctica's cold climate. Snow and ice cover 98 percent of the land. During summer, small areas of snow melt, giving water to snow-covered algae. The water helps red **algae** bloom under the snow, making the snow look pink.

Most plants grow only along Antarctica's snow-free coast. Antarctic hair grass and Antarctic pearlworts live on this warmer land. Green moss and bright orange **lichens** cover rocks.

◀ During summer, more than 300 types of algae, including red algae, grow in Antarctica's cold climate.

Animals

Many ocean animals live in the water around Antarctica, but few visit the icy land. Seals and penguins spend a few months on land raising their young. Waterproof feathers and a layer of fat keep penguins dry and warm. Small animals called mites and ticks live on seals and penguins.

During summer, more than 40 types of birds, including petrels and skuas, nest on Antarctica. During the day, they fly over the Southern Ocean looking for fish to eat.

◄ Emperor penguins waddle slowly across the cold, icy land. Strong claws help them grip the ice.

Claims on Antarctica

SOUTH ATLANTIC
OCEAN

INDIAN
OCEAN

SOUTHERN
OCEAN

UNITED KINGDOM CLAIM

NORWEGIAN CLAIM

ARCTIC CIRCLE

ARGENTINE CLAIM

SOUTH POLE

CHILEAN CLAIM

AUSTRALIAN CLAIM

SOUTHERN
OCEAN

FRENCH CLAIM

AUSTRALIAN CLAIM

SOUTH PACIFIC
OCEAN

NEW ZEALAND
CLAIM

Claims

Unlike other continents, Antarctica is not divided into separate countries. Seven countries claim to own parts of Antarctica. Australia has the biggest claim. Argentina, Chile, New Zealand, Norway, France, and the United Kingdom also have claims. Many countries without claims have research stations on Antarctica.

Most of the world has signed the Antarctic **Treaty**. This treaty says countries can only use Antarctica for peaceful reasons.

THE UNITED STATES OF AMERICA
WELCOMES YOU TO
AMUNDSEN – SCOTT SOUTH POLE STATION

People

Antarctica has no **native** people. Visitors travel to Antarctica by riding in ships or airplanes. Scientists from many different countries stay in Antarctica while doing research. They live in research stations, which are like big houses. Scientists study Antarctica's plants, animals, and landforms.

For the summer months, about 4,000 researchers stay in Antarctica. During the cold winter, only about 1,000 people stay in Antarctica. A growing number of **tourists** also visit Antarctica each year.

◄ In Antarctica, scientists stay at the Amundsen-Scott South Pole Station and other research stations.

Living in Antarctica

Life in Antarctica is harsh. Even in summer, the continent stays windy, dry, and cold. Scientists wear many layers of clothing to stay warm. In summer, researchers may have trouble sleeping for a few weeks. During these weeks, it's light for about 20 hours a day.

Scientists sleep and eat at research stations. Some vegetables are grown at Antarctica's research stations inside greenhouses. But most food must be flown or shipped to this cold continent.

◄ Goggles and layers of clothing help protect researchers from Antarctica's freezing temperatures.

Antarctica and the World

People from all over the world are interested in Antarctica's unique climate. Thousands of researchers travel to Antarctica each year. This continent's snow-covered land holds clues about the world's history and future.

Scientists test Antarctica's old ice sheets to learn about past climates. These ice sheets also help predict the future world climate. Research in Antarctica may help solve future world problems. Today, Antarctica's unique land is being carefully **protected**.

◀ At the South Pole, a scientist collects samples of Antarctica's ice, snow, and air.

Glossary

algae (AL-jee)—small plants without roots or stems that grow in water or on damp surfaces

climate (KLYE-mit)—the usual weather in a place

coast (KOHST)—land that is next to an ocean or a sea

lichen (LYE-ken)—a flat, mosslike growth on rocks and trees

native (NAY-tiv)—originally from a certain place

protect (pruh-TECT)—to guard or to keep something safe from harm

research (REE-surch)—the process of studying and learning about a subject

tourist (TOOR-ist)—someone who travels and visits places for fun, relaxation, or adventure

treaty (TREE-tee)—an official agreement between two or more groups or countries

Read More

Mattern, Joanne. *Antarctica: World's Biggest Glacier.*
Nature's Greatest Hits. New York: PowerKids Press, 2002.

Rau, Dana Meachen. *Antarctica.* Geography of the World.
Chanhassen, Minn.: Child's World, 2004.

Internet Sites

FactHound offers a safe, fun way to
find Internet sites related to this book.
All of the sites on FactHound have been
researched by our staff.

Here's how:
1. Visit *www.facthound.com*
2. Type in this special code **0736854266** for
   age-appropriate sites. Or enter a search word
   related to this book for a more general search.
3. Click on the **Fetch It** button.

FactHound will fetch the best sites for you!

Index